INVESTMENT INSIGHTS
Decoding Mutual Fund Investment & Retirement Realities

Subrata Das Gupta

This book is dedicated to
my father

Table of Contents

Table of Contents

Table of Contents

Chapter

Inspirational Quotes on Investing

"Risk comes from not knowing what you are doing."

– Warren Buffett

"The desire to become a millionaire overnight is the root cause of failures in the stock market!"

– Vijay Kedia

"The best investment you can make, is an investment in yourself...

The more you learn,

The more you'll earn"

– Warren Buffett.

"More important than the how we achieve financial freedom, is the why. Find your reasons why you want to be free and wealthy."

– Robert Kiyosaki

"Understanding the calculation of financial ratios is crucial, but the true significance lies in utilizing these ratios effectively to select the optimal funds for our investments."

— **Subrata Das Gupta.**

"Simply relying on SIP won't take you anywhere; instead, focus on acquiring new skills to cultivate extra part-time income at the beginning of your career."

— **Subrata Das Gupta.**

Chapter

Understanding Your Risk Appetite

RISKOMETER
MEDIUM
LOW
HIGH

Before proceeding with any investment, it's crucial to assess your risk profile thoroughly. Each investor possesses a unique risk profile determined by age, financial objectives, income level, and existing commitments. Familiarizing yourself with the following common risk profiles can help you make informed investment decisions:

1. Aggressive

2. Moderately Aggressive

3. Moderate

4. Moderately Conservative

5. Conservative

Understanding these risk profiles empowers individuals to align their investments with their specific financial goals and risk tolerance.

Chapter

Salary Management Strategies

Monthly take home salary		40,000		
Needs (50%)	Wants (20%)	Savings & Investments (30%)		
20,000	8,000	12,000		
Food	Entertainment			
Groceries	Shopping			
Housing/Rent	Dining out			
Utilities/bills	Hobbies			
Transportation	vacation			
Health insurance (Section 80D)	Consumer Electronics etc			
Term insurance etc.:- Only for earning members of family. Amount of insurance cover must be 15 times of your annual expenditure	Some money of this portion can be used for paying off our large debt, if any or can be deployed to fulfill our needs			

Monthly take home salary	40,000	w				
Needs (50%)	Wants (20%)	Savings & Investments (30%)				
20,000	8,000					12,000
Food	Entertainment	Retirement planning investments (15%)	Tax Savings investments (15%)	Goal- Based investing (70%)		
Groceries	Shopping	PPF or NPS	NPS, PPF, SSY, ELSS fund & NSC etc.	Short-term goals (1-3 years)	Mid- term goals (03-06 years)	Long- term goals (06 years onwards)

Housing/Rent	Dining out	1,800	1,800	Liquid fund, bank FD, RD, Money market fund, ultra short term fund & short term fund etc.	Hybrid mutual fund, ELSS, corporate bond fund & Medium term fund etc.	Shares (Direct equity), equity Mutual fund, International equity Mutual fund, Banking and PSU fund, Dynamic bond fund & Gold etc.)

Utilities/bills	Hobbies	Here I am omitting other investment instruments such as EPF and GPF because they are accessible only to specific groups:	Most tax saving instruments offer more than just tax benefits. They also function as important schemes that build up a corpus to meet your mid- term &	8,400
Transportation	vacation			
Health insurance (Section 80D)	Consumer Electronics etc			
Term insurance etc:- Only for earning members of family. Amount of insurance cover must be 15 times of	Some money of this portion can be used for paying off our large debt, if any or can be deployed to fulfill our needs			

your annual expenditure		EPF is exclusive to employees of companies registered under the EPF Act, and GPF is reserved for government employees as a mandatory	ong- term financial goals. Many of these tax- saving instruments are government - backed, which means that they are legitimate, transparent and	

		provision. However, PPF and NPS are open to all Indian citizens regardless of profession.	Idependable investments.	

Note: - before starting our investment journey, it is recommended to maintain an emergency fund equivalent to 6 months' worth of our expenses. This fund should ideally be kept in either a savings bank account or a liquid fund for easy accessibility in times of need.

Chapter

Introduction to Mutual Funds

- A mutual fund is a company that brings together money from many people and the fund manager of that company invests that money in stocks, bonds, debentures, or other assets. After deducting fees typically ranging from 1% to 1.5%, the collective returns generated from these investments are distributed among the investors in proportion to their investment amounts.

Cons of Investing in Mutual Funds in India

Lack of control: Investing in a mutual fund means giving up control over individual investment decisions. The fund manager has the authority to buy and sell assets within the fund, which may not always align with your specific financial goals or risk tolerance. This loss of control can be a disadvantage for investors who prefer a more hands-on approach to managing their investments.

Fees and expenses: One of the most significant drawbacks of mutual funds is the fees and expenses associated with them. These costs can reduce your overall returns and diminish the benefits of your investments. Mutual funds may impose various fees, such as management fees, administrative fees, and load charges. Therefore, it's important to carefully review a fund's expense ratio and sales charges to understand their impact on your investment returns over time.

Possible underperformance: There's a possibility that the fund's return may not always exceed the market or meet your expectations.

Chapter

Types of Mutual Funds

Types of Equity Mutual Funds

- **Large-Cap:** As per SEBI circular for Mutual Fund schemes, the companies ranked from the 1st to 100th in terms of market capitalization are known as large-cap fund. Check Nifty 100 index for the list.

- **Mid Cap:** The companies ranked from the 101 to 250 in terms of market capitalization are known as midcap fund. Check the Nifty Midcap 150 index for the list.

- **Small-Cap:** The companies ranked from the 251st position onwards in terms of market capitalization are known as small-cap funds. Check the Nifty Small-Cap 250 index for the list.

- **Multi-cap Fund:** Multi-cap funds are equity funds with a minimum equity exposure of 75%. Following SEBI's new guidelines, multi-cap funds must allocate at least 25% of their portfolio to each market capitalization category.

- **Flexi-cap Fund:** Flexi-cap funds are equity funds with a minimum equity exposure of 65%. They invest in equities across market capitalizations without a fixed allocation. Fund managers have the flexibility to adjust asset allocation based on market conditions, often leaning toward large-cap stocks for stability.

- **Focused Fund:** Focused mutual funds are a type of equity fund that concentrates investments in a limited number of stocks, typically up to 30, as per SEBI guidelines. Similar to multi-cap funds, they can invest across market segments: large-cap, midcap, or small-cap.

- Value funds: Value funds follow a value investing strategy, targeting stocks perceived to be undervalued based on fundamental characteristics.

- **Contra Fund:** Contra mutual funds invest against prevailing market trends, often purchasing stocks that are currently underperforming. Fund managers take a contrarian approach, favoring stocks ignored by investors or those experiencing excessive demand. While potentially offering long-term gains, these funds are not suited for short-term investments.

- **Sectorial or Thematic funds:** These funds are considered high-risk investments as they predominantly focus on specific sectors. Any adverse changes in the macro or micro economy, business regulations, consumer behavior, or technology can significantly impact investments.

- **ELSS Fund:** ELSS funds are equity funds investing a minimum of 80% in equity and equity-related instruments. They diversify investments across market capitalizations, themes, and sectors. ELSS funds have a lock-in period of 3 years, with tax exemption under section 80C of the Income Tax Act and LTCG taxation as per prevailing rules.

Types of Debt Mutual Funds

- **Overnight Fund:** Invest in 1-day maturity securities. Can expect a 2-3 % annualized return.

- **Liquid and Money Market Fund:** Invest in treasury bills maturing within 90 days. Can expect a 5-6% annualized return.

- **Ultra Short-term Fund:** Invest in treasury bills and commercial papers maturing in 3-6 months. Can expect a 6-7% annualized return.

- **Low Duration Fund:** Invest in securities maturing within 6-12 months.

- **Short-term Fund:** Invest in commercial papers, commercial deposits, and corporate bonds with 1-3 years of maturity. Can expect a 6.5 - 7.5% annualized return.

- **Medium-term Fund:** Invest in commercial papers, commercial deposits, corporate bonds, and debentures with 3-4 years of maturity. Can expect a 7.5 - 8.5% annualized return.

- **Long-term Fund:** Invest in corporate bonds, debentures and govt. securities with more than 07 years maturity. Can expect 8 - 8.5% annualized return.

- **Dynamic Bond:** Invest in debt and money market instruments across duration.

- **Corporate Bond Fund:** Investing in the highest-rated corporate bonds (80% of total assets).

- **Credit Risk Fund:-** Investing in below highest-rated corporate bonds (65% of total assets)

- **Banking and PSU Fund:** Investing in debt instruments of banks, public sector undertakings, and public financial institutions (80% of total assets).

- **Gilt Fund:** Investing in government securities across duration (80% of total assets).

- **Gilt 10 Years:** Investing in government securities having maturity of 10 years (80% of total assets).

- **Floater Fund:** Investing in floating rate instruments (65% of total assets). In a regular bond investment, we receive a fixed interest payment at regular intervals as long as we own that bond. In a floating rate bond, the interest rate that we receive is not fixed. They are linked to benchmarks like REPO, G-Sec rate, or MIBOR. Interest amounts change according to the changes in the benchmark rate. If the benchmark rate increases, you get higher returns, and if the benchmark rate reduces, you get lower returns. An example of a floating rate bond is the RBI floating rate bond, which is currently offering 7.15%. This 7.15% is not fixed. Rate of interest = NSC rate + 0.35%. The current NSC interest rate is 6.8%. If the NSC rate changes to 6.5%, then the RBI bond new rate will be 6.5% + 0.35) = 6.85%.

Types of Hybrid Mutual Funds

- **Conservative Hybrid Fund:** Investment in equity and equity-related instruments (between 10- 25% of total assets). Investment in Debt instruments (between 75 - 90% of total assets).

- **Balanced Hybrid Fund:** Investment in equity and equity-related instruments (between 40-60% of total assets). Investment in Debt instruments (between 40-60% of total assets).

- **Aggressive Hybrid Fund:** Investment in equity and equity-related instruments (between 65-80% of total assets).

Investment in Debt instruments (between 20- 35% of total assets).

- **Dynamic Asset Allocation Fund or Balanced Advantage Fund:** Fund managers can allocate their money between debt and equity as per their choice. It is not such a fix.

- **Arbitrage Fund:** In an arbitrage fund, the fund manager simultaneously buys shares in the cash market and sells them in futures or derivatives markets. The difference in the cost price and the selling price is the return we earn. It is the safest investment option but with low returns.

- **Multi-Asset Allocation Fund:** Invest in at least 3 asset classes with a minimum allocation of at least 10% each in all 3 asset classes. The asset allocation of these funds generally includes securities across equity, debt markets, gold, real estate, and so on.

Chapter

Understanding the Differences: Direct vs. Regular Mutual Fund Plans

a) **Direct Plan:** Direct Mutual Funds are offered directly by the AMC or fund house without the involvement of third-party agents, brokers, or distributors.

b) **Regular Plan:** Investments in mutual funds are made through mutual fund agents or banks in a Regular Plan. This option incurs additional fees, with the expense ratio typically 0.5% to 1% higher than that of a Direct Plan. Furthermore, tracking the performance of a Regular Plan is not possible.

Can I switch from a regular to a direct plan?

- Yes, it is possible to switch from a regular plan to a direct plan. There are numerous apps available on the Google Play Store that facilitates this transition seamlessly. For instance, the IND Money app offers such functionality. In my opinion, opting for a direct plan is preferable over a regular plan, particularly if one possesses sufficient knowledge about mutual fund investments.

Chapter

Investing in Mutual Funds: App Recommendations

1. Groww

Among the array of investment apps available, Groww stands out as a commendable option for mutual fund investment. Established in 2016, Groww boasts a strong rating on the Play Store, making it a trustworthy platform for users. One of its key attractions is its fee structure: there are no account opening charges, no Annual Maintenance Charges (AMC), and no buying or selling fees for mutual funds. Moreover, Groww allows investment in Direct Mutual Funds, which can potentially result in higher returns due to lower expense ratios. Security is prioritized through its association with CDSL, and users can avail of the nomination facility for added peace of mind. The platform offers convenient features like a monthly SIP facility, bank mandate setup, external fund tracking, and options for Systematic Transfer Plan (STP) and Systematic Withdrawal Plan (SWP). Users also praise Groww for its excellent customer support, clean user interface, and seamless switching between regular and direct plans.

2. IND Money:

IND Money stands out as an excellent choice, particularly for those interested in global funds. Notably, it offers robust features allowing users to effectively manage and track various financial aspects, ranging from daily expenses to investments and even credit scores.

Chapter

Dealing with Mutual Fund App Shutdowns

These apps serve solely as intermediaries for our investments. Even if we invest through these apps, our funds are ultimately directed to asset management companies (AMCs) such as HDFC, ICICI, etc., where we have made our investments. Therefore, in the event these apps close down, we can still access our funds by visiting the respective AMC's website with the help of our folio number, which was allotted to us at the time of investment.

Chapter

Tax Implications of Mutual Fund Investments

Equity: Returns from equity mutual funds are subject to taxation based on the duration of the investment. If redeemed before one year, Short-Term Capital Gains (STCG) are applicable at a rate of 15%. For investments held beyond one year, the Long-Term Capital Gains (LTCG) tax is levied at 10% on returns exceeding Rs. 1 lakh in a financial year.

Debt: Unlike equity funds, debt mutual funds are not categorized into short-term and long-term for taxation purposes. Instead, gains from debt funds are taxed according to an individual's income tax slab.

Chapter

Strategies to Minimize Capital Gains Tax

Tax harvesting is a strategy where you sell a portion of your Equity Mutual Fund holdings annually to realize long-term gains. Afterward, you reinvest the proceeds back into the same fund.

To grasp this concept more clearly, consider the following example: Assume you initially invested Rs. 6 lakh in an Equity Fund on February 1, 2021, and achieved a 12% return on your investment. Now, by March 1, 2022, your investment's returns and capital gains would resemble the following:

Lump-Sum Investment on 1st February 2021	Rs. 6 lakh
Return Generated (Quarterly compounded)	12%
Investment Value on 1st March 2022	Rs. 6.75 lakh
Long Term Capital Gains on 1st March 2022	Rs. 75,305

If you cash out your investments on 1st March 2022, you won't owe any Capital Gains Tax because your gains amount to Rs. 75,305, and gains up to Rs. 1 lakh in a financial year are exempt from tax. After that, you'll need to put the money back into the same scheme. On investing the proceeds, i.e., Rs. 6.75 lakh on 2nd March 2022 and assuming returns of 12% p.a. on your investment, your investment will grow to something like this by 5th March 2023.

Initial Lump Sum Investment on 2nd March 2022	Rs. 6.75 lakh
Return Generated (Quarterly compounded)	12% p.a.
Investment Value on 5th March 2023	Rs. 7.60 lakh
Long-Term Capital Gains on 20th March 2023	Rs. 84,718

Now, when you redeem your investments again, they qualify as Long-Term Capital Gains since they have been held for over a year. However, you won't owe any tax because the capital gains amount to Rs. 84,718, which falls below the Rs. 1 lakh limit for the financial year.

Now, consider a case where instead of redeeming your investment in March 2022, you stayed invested and let your Rs. 6 lakh initial investment grow till 5th March 2023.

Initial Lump Sum Investment on 1st February 2021	Rs. 6 lakh
Return (Quarterly compounded)	12% p.a.
Investment Value on 5th March 2023	Rs. 7.60 lakh
Total Long-Term Capital Gains on 20th March 2023	Rs. 1.60 lakh
Taxable Long-Term Capital Gains on 20th March 2023	Rs. 60,000
Capital Gains Tax Payable (at 10%)	Rs. 6,000

As you can observe, tax harvesting enabled you to avoid paying Capital Gains Tax on your Mutual Fund investments.

Tax harvesting can also be utilized when investing through the SIP (Systematic Investment Plan) method. You just need to redeem units eligible for long-term capital gains, which are held for 12 months or more, and reinvest the proceeds each time. However, the process can be somewhat complex.

Misconception about tax harvesting: Tax harvesting does not interfere with the compounding effect in mutual funds.

Chapter

Loans Against Mutual Fund Investments

- Individuals, NRIs, firms, HUFs, trusts, companies etc. are eligible to obtain a loan against their mutual fund investments. Minors are the only exception.

- To secure a loan against mutual funds, investors can approach banks or financial institutions and submit their application. Many finance companies offer online applications, streamlining the entire process and providing instant approval.

- The interest rates for loans against mutual funds are typically lower compared to personal loans due to the presence of collateral. Processing fees and foreclosure charges are usually minimal.

- For equity mutual funds, borrowers can typically access up to 50% of the net asset value, while fixed income mutual funds may allow loans of 70–80% of the net asset value.

- Some banks may limit lending to specific mutual fund schemes. For instance, SBI may only offer loans against mutual schemes from SBI Mutual Fund.

- When pledging mutual fund units for a loan, the units remain invested in the market. Pledged units are only sold by the bank in the event of default. As long as the borrower does not default, investments remain linked to the market, allowing continued earnings.

Chapter

Compounding Theory and Mutual Funds

COLLEGE
$
POWER OF
COMPOUNDING

1. Does a Mutual Fund operate according to the principles of compounding theory?

Answer: No.

Reasons: a) Mutual funds do not offer fixed or guaranteed returns.

b) Mutual funds may yield negative returns at times.

c) The Compound Annual Growth Rate (CAGR) returns displayed by Mutual Funds are merely indicative averages and do not assure guaranteed returns.

d) No mutual fund company provides any commitments regarding compounding returns in writing.

2. Why does compounding apply to bank FD/RD?

Reasons: a) Bank FD or RD offers fixed positive returns regularly, with no negative returns.

b) The Compound Annual Growth Rate (CAGR) returns are predetermined in FD/RD investments.

c) Bank FD or RD consistently offers compound interest options, be it quarterly, half-yearly, or annually.

Conclusion: - Even though no mutual fund company promises compounding returns in writing but the stock market usually performs consistently over time.

Chapter

SIP vs Lump Sum Investment

- The comparison between SIP (Systematic Investment Plan) and lump-sum investments is not straightforward and is heavily reliant on individual circumstances and objectives. SIP is more suitable for individuals with consistent cash flows, while lump-sum investments are ideal for those with a significant amount of funds available at once and without a regular income stream. Additionally, this comparison is inherently biased because the time horizon for investment growth differs between the 2 modes.

Chapter

Mutual Fund SIP Frequency and Ideal Date

- Research indicates that the frequency of SIPs, whether daily, weekly, or monthly, does not significantly affect returns. However, opting for daily or weekly SIPs may pose challenges in monitoring your investments compared to monthly SIPs. For convenience, consider aligning SIP dates with your salary if you receive a fixed monthly income.

- Studies indicate that the timing of SIP investments, whether at the end, middle, or beginning of the month, does not significantly affect returns. Opting for the beginning of the month aligns with many individuals' salary receipts, facilitating the prioritization of investments over discretionary spending. However, it's important to note that failing to make payments for 3 consecutive months may result in the automatic cancellation of your SIP in mutual funds.

Chapter

Stopping and Modifying SIPs of Mutual Funds

Yes, we can stop our SIP in MF anytime, without paying any penalty. The Groww app facilitates easy cancellation of SIPs. When we cancel our mutual fund SIP, the monthly amount will no longer be debited from our bank account. However, the invested amount remains in the fund and continues to accrue returns until a redemption request is made. It's important to be mindful of any exit loads that are applicable in such cases.

The Groww app also allows for easy editing or skipping of SIP installments. If adjustments or changes are desired, they should be made at least 2 working days prior to the next installment to ensure timely processing. Otherwise, the modifications may take effect after the upcoming installment date. Furthermore, it is possible to skip only one installment at a time, and there is no limit on the number of times a SIP can be edited or skipped. Additionally, there are no hidden charges associated with modifying SIPs. We can't decrease the SIP amount.

Chapter

Mutual Fund Categories to Avoid

Here are 5 Mutual Fund categories that you might consider avoiding:

A) **Sectorial or Thematic Funds:** These funds are deemed high-risk investments as they predominantly invest in a specific sector. Any adverse changes in the sector, whether due to macro or microeconomic shifts, altered business regulations, or changes in consumer behavior or technology, can significantly impact investments.

B) **Small-Cap Funds:** These funds are highly volatile and risky compared to large-cap equity-oriented funds. Small-cap stocks often face liquidity constraints due to their smaller capital base.

C) **NFO (New Fund Offer):** These funds lack a past track record and typically come with higher expenses.

D) Gilt Funds: While these funds don't carry credit risk, they are primarily susceptible to interest rate risk.

E) Aggressive Hybrid, Balanced Hybrid, and Equity Savings Funds: In my opinion, investors should personally allocate their funds between debt and equity according to their risk appetite and suitability. It's advisable to maintain a clear separation between risky and non-risky allocations and keep the investment strategy simple.

Chapter

Preferred Mutual Fund Categories

As previously mentioned, every investor should ideally have a maximum of 6 funds in their portfolio, with 4 equity and 2 debt funds. Considering my moderately conservative risk profile, here are my favorite categories:

a) Large-Cap Fund

b) Flexi-Cap Fund

c) International Fund

d) Midcap Fund

e) Banking and PSU Fund

f) Dynamic Bond Fund or Corporate bond Fund

Note: Each of the above categories should have a maximum allocation of one fund. Furthermore, our investment horizon for equity and debt funds should exceed 6 years. For short-term goals, I typically opt for bank FDs and RDs.

Chapter

Selecting Debt Mutual Funds

Different Parameters

1. AUM (Asset under Management): In case of debt mutual fund, high AUM can / may increase the returns.

2. Sharpe Ratio: Choose a mutual fund with a higher Sharpe ratio.

3. Beta: it measures the volatility of the mutual fund portfolio compared to the benchmark index. Choose a mutual fund with a lower beta.

4. Standard Deviation: Choose a mutual fund with a lower standard deviation for lower risk.

5. Alpha: It's the extra return over and above the benchmark return on a risk-adjusted basis. Choose a mutual fund with a higher alpha.

6. Choose a mutual fund with a higher sortino ratio.

7. Higher Macaulay duration, average maturity, and modified duration of a debt fund compared with its peers indicate that the fund has higher interest rate sensitivity.

8. The expense ratio means the fee charged by the fund house for their services. The maximum limit of expense ratio as per SEBI for debt funds is 2.25% per annum. Choose a mutual fund with a lower expense ratio.

9. YTM (Yield to maturity): Expected total rate of return if the bond is held until maturity. A high YTM may be indicative of higher credit and liquidity risk.

10. Exit loads: When we invest for the long term, the exit load automatically

becomes nil. However, in the case of short-term investment (less than one year), one must look for mutual fund schemes that have a minimal exit load.

Example 1

Let's consider selecting the best fund from the ultra-short-term category. After evaluating four and 5-star ratings provided by both Value Research and Morning Star, along with prioritizing funds with higher Asset under Management (AUM), we've identified 4 contenders: ABC, DEF, GHI, and JKL funds. Now, our focus shifts to comparing these funds based on various risk parameters and other essential factors. It's crucial to acknowledge that any debt fund inherently carries 3 types of risks: credit risk, interest rate risk, and liquidity risk. With this understanding, let's proceed to compare the funds.

Sl. No	Different parameters	Name of the funds				My preference
		ABC	DEF	GHI	JKL	
1.	AUM (in Cr.)	18,972	9,692	12,698	5,680	
2.	Alpha	3.73	3.33	3.60	3.31	
3.	Beta	0.83	1.16	1.07	1.43	
4.	Expense ratio	0.30	0.34	0.33	0.39	
5.	Sharpe ratio	4.06	3.44	3.71	3.26	ABC
6.	Standard Deviation	0.70	0.80	0.75	0.85	
7.	Sortino	7.64	6.84	7.27	6.76	GHI
8.	Modified duration	0.30	0.41	0.36	0.52	
9..	Macaulay Duration	0.33	0.52	0.36	0.54	
10.	Average maturity	0.37	0.53	0.40	0.56	
11.	Average credit quality	AAA	AAA	AAA	AAA	
12.	YTM	4.29	4.26	4.06	3.94	
13.	Style box(credit quality and Interest rate sensitivity)	CQ=H & IRS=L	CQ=H & IRS=L	CQ=H & IRS=L	CQ=H & IRS=L	

Sl. No	Different parameters	Name of the funds				My preference
		ABC	DEF	GHI	JKL	
14.	Number of Securities(Should have at least 40)	97	156	82	68	
15.	Exit load	Nil	Nil	Nil	Nil	
16.	Fund management	No recent change in management	No recent change in management	No recent change in management	No recent change in management	DEF
17.	Fund's past 10 years performance in comparison with its benchmark	Very good	Very good	Very good	Very good	JKL
18.	Port folio Analysis (risk profile of the instruments in which the fund has invested & must have less exposure in below 'AA' rated bonds)	Good	Good	Good	Good	

Note:- We can readily obtain the aforementioned details from the fund's factsheet, accessible on the Value Research and Morningstar websites.

Example 2

In the second scenario, our aim is to identify the top-performing fund from the Banking and PSU Category. Following a similar approach to the previous example, we have shortlisted 3 banking and PSU funds based on their 4 and five-star ratings from Value Research and Morningstar, as well as their higher Asset under Management (AUM). These funds are ABC, DEF, and XYZ. Now, our focus shifts to conducting a comparative analysis, considering various risk parameters and other relevant factors, to determine the optimal choice among them.

Sl. No	Different parameters	Name of the funds			My preference
		ABC	DEF	XYZ	
1.	AUM (in Cr.)	6,697	19,205	15,823	1) DEF
2.	Alpha	6.13	7.43	6.91	2) XYZ
3.	Beta	3.07	1.97	2.49	3) ABC
4.	Expense ratio	0.34	0.31	0.33	
5.	Sharpe ratio	2.27	2.45	2.33	
6.	Standard Deviation	2.38	2.17	2.20	
7.	Sortino	3.89	4.85	4.18	
8.	Modified duration	2.40	1.35	2.00	
9..	Macaulay Duration	2.38	1.41	2.01	
10.	Average maturity	3.49	1.51	2.76	
11.	Average credit quality	AAA	AAA	AAA	
12.	YTM	4.93	4.49	4.95	
13.	Style box(credit quality and Interest rate sensitivity)	CQ=H & IRS=M	CQ=H & IRS=M	CQ=H & IRS=M	

Sl. No	Different parameters	Name of the funds			My preference
		ABC	DEF	XYZ	
14.	Number of Securities (Should have at least 40)	103	191	253	
15.	Exit load	NIL	NIL	NIL	
16.	Fund management	No recent change in fund management.	No recent change in fund management.	No recent change in fund management.	
17.	Fund's past 10 years performance in comparison with its benchmark	Very good	Very good	Very good	
18.	Port folio Analysis (risk profile of the instruments in which the fund has invested & must have less exposure in below 'AA' rated bonds)	Very good	Very good	Very good	

Example 3

In our final example, we aim to select the optimal fund from the liquid category. Following our customary approach, we have chosen 4 liquid funds based on their 4 and 5-star ratings from Value Research and Morningstar, as well as their higher Asset under Management (AUM). These funds are ABC, DEF, GHI, and OPQ. Now, our task is to conduct a comprehensive comparison of these funds, considering various risk parameters and other relevant factors, to determine the most suitable option.

Sl. No	Different parameters	Name of the funds				My preference
		ABC	DEF	GHI	OPQ	
1.	AUM (in Cr.)	21,654	28,554	9,608	34,592	
2.	Alpha	1.77	1.80	1.76	1.81	
3.	Beta	1.09	1.09	1.12	1.08	
4.	Expense ratio	0.20	0.18	0.21	0.11	
5.	Sharpe ratio	2.19	2.21	2.16	2.22	**1) OPQ**
6.	Standard Deviation	0.51	0.51	0.52	0.50	
7.	Sortino	8.03	8.13	7.62	8.43	**2) DEF**
8.	Modified duration	0.10	0.09	0.15	0.03	
9.	Macaulay Duration	0.10	0.09	0.14	0.03	
10.	Average maturity	0.10	0.10	0.15	0.03	
11.	Average credit quality	AAA	AAA	AAA	AAA	
12.	YTM	3.51	3.26	3.57	3.41	

Sl. No	Different parameters	Name of the funds				My preference
		ABC	DEF	GHI	OPQ	
13.	Style box(credit quality and Interest rate sensitivity)	CQ=H & IRS=L	CQ=H & IRS=L	CQ=H & IRS=L	CQ=H & IRS=L	
14.	Number of Securities(Should have at least 40)	103	62	103	41	**3) ABC**
15.	Exit load	No exit load after 6 days	No exit load after 6 days	No exit load after 6 days	No exit load after 6 days	**4) GHI**
16.	Fund management	No recent change in fund management	No recent change in fund management	No recent change in fund management	No recent change in fund management	

Sl. No	Different parameters	Name of the funds				My preference
		ABC	DEF	GHI	OPQ	
17.	Fund's past 10 years performance in comparison with its benchmark	Very good	Very good	Very good	Very good	
18.	Port folio Analysis (risk profile of the instruments in which the fund has invested & must have less exposure in below 'AA' rated bonds)	Very good	Very good	Very good	Very good	

Chapter

Selecting Equity Mutual Funds

Different Parameters

a) **Alpha**: This measures the excess return of a fund compared to its benchmark on a risk-adjusted basis. Opt for funds with a higher alpha.

b) **Beta**: Choose funds with lower beta, as it indicates lower volatility compared to the benchmark index.

c) **Standard Deviation**: Lower standard deviation signifies lower risk. Hence, I prefer funds with a lower standard deviation.

d) **Sortino Ratio**: Prioritize funds with a higher Sortino ratio, which considers downside risk in its calculation.

e) **Sharpe Ratio**: Select funds with a higher Sharpe ratio, indicating better risk-adjusted returns.

f) **R-Squared**: Ensure that the R-squared value of any fund exceeds 80, reflecting a strong correlation between the fund and its benchmark.

g) **Turnover Ratio**: Opt for funds with a lower turnover ratio, indicating less frequent buying and selling of stocks by the fund manager.

h) **Maximum Drawdown**: Choose funds with a lower maximum drawdown to mitigate potential losses during market downturns.

i) **Expense Ratio**: The expense ratio reflects the fee charged by the fund house. Choose funds with a lower expense ratio, ensuring they stay within the SEBI-mandated limit of 2.5% per annum for equity funds.

j) **Exit loads:** - When we invest for the long term, the exit load automatically becomes nil. However, in the case of short-term investment (less than one year), one must look for mutual fund schemes that have a minimal exit load.

k) Choose a mutual fund with a lower P/E ratio, provided that all the funds follow same style of investing.

l) Choose a mutual fund with a lower P/B ratio, provided that all the funds follow the same style of investing.

Example 1

Suppose we aim to choose the top-performing fund from the large-cap category. To this end, we've shortlisted 3 large-cap funds, namely ABC, DEF, and OPQ, based on their 4 and

5-star ratings awarded by Value Research and Morningstar. Our next step involves a comprehensive comparison of these funds, considering various risk parameters and other relevant factors. Despite reaching a considerable size, a large fund might still maintain its strong performance.

Sl. No	Different parameters	Name of the funds			My preference
		ABC	DEF	OPQ	
1.	AUM (in Cr.)	19,153	4,701	33,153	
2.	Alpha	4.70	3.49	1.35	
3.	Beta	0.77	0.86	1.02	
4.	Expense ratio	0.55	0.55	0.82	
5.	Sharpe ratio	0.47	0.40	0.26	
6.	Standard Deviation	17.69	19.06	23.06	
7.	Sortino	1.19	1.17	0.89	1) ABC
8.	R2 (should be more than 80)	89.11	97.53	95.29	
9..	Drawdown (maximum)	-19.35	-21.91	27.42	2) DEF
10.	Turnover ratio	23	36	45	
11.	Style box	Style-G/Cap-L	Style-G/Cap-L	Style-G/Cap-L	
12	Number of Stocks in a scheme	34	50	62	
13.	Exit load	1% for redemption within 365 days.	1% for redemption within 365 days	1% for redemption within 365 days	

Sl. No	Different parameters	Name of the funds			My preference
		ABC	DEF	OPQ	
14.	Fund management	No recent change in fund management.	No recent change in fund management.	There is a recent change in fund management.	
15.	Fund's past 05 years trailing returns in comparison with its benchmark	Very good	Very good	Good	3) OPQ
16.	Rolling returns	Very good	Very good	Very good	
17.	Fund's P/E ratio (only if all the above mentioned funds follow same style of investing, whether it be growth or value. Otherwise, it may not be relevant for comparison.	25.27	25.74	26.66	

Sl. No	Different parameters	Name of the funds			My preference
		ABC	DEF	OPQ	
18.	Fund's P/B ratio (only if all the above mentioned funds follow same style of investing, whether it be growth or value. Otherwise, it may not be relevant for comparison.	3.61	3.68	4.09	

Note:- We can readily obtain the aforementioned details from the fund's factsheet, accessible on the Value Research and Morningstar websites.

Example 2

In the second example, our focus is on selecting the optimal fund within the flexi-cap category. Following the 4 and 5-star ratings provided by Value Research and Morningstar, we have identified 4 funds within this category: ABC, DEF, OPQ, and XYZ funds. Our next step involves a thorough comparison of these funds, taking into account various risk parameters and other pertinent factors.

Sl. No	Different parameters	Name of the funds				My preference
		ABC	DEF	OPQ	XYZ	
1.	AUM (in Cr.)	6,393	7,451	3,056	14,861	
2.	Alpha	7.68	6.97	6.82	4.19	
3.	Beta	0.74	0.76	0.85	0.97	
4.	Expense ratio	0.54	0.84	0.99	1.25	
5.	Sharpe ratio	0.59	0.56	0.50	0.41	
6.	Standard Deviation	18	18.44	19.81	22.75	
7.	Sortino	1.27	1.20	1.07	1.02	ABC
8.	R2 (should be more than 80)	85	88	97	96	DEF
9..	Drawdown (maximum)	-18.98	-22.26	-23.13	-26.09	
10.	Turnover ratio	6.25	12	68	133	
11.	Style box	Style-G/Cap-L	Style-G/Cap-L	Style-G/Cap-L	Style-G/Cap-L	
12.	No of Stocks in a portfolio	28	37	58	60	

Sl. No	Different parameters	Name of the funds				My preference
		ABC	DEF	OPQ	XYZ	
13.	Exit load	1% for redemption within 12 months	1% for redemption within 12 months	1% for redemption within 12 months	1% for redemption within 12 months	
14.	Fund management	No recent change in management.	No recent change in management	No recent change in management	No recent change in management	OPQ
15.	Fund's past 05 years trailing returns in comparison with its benchmark	Very good	Good	Above average	average	XYZ
16.	Rolling returns	Very good	Good	Above average	average	

Sl. No	Different parameters	Name of the funds				My preference
		ABC	DEF	OPQ	XYZ	
17.	Fund's P/E ratio (only if all the above mentioned funds follow same style of investing, whether it be growth or value. Otherwise, it may not be relevant for comparison.	26.12	35.07	40.65	45.30	
18.	Fund's P/B ratio (only if all the above mentioned funds follow same style of investing, whether it be growth or value. Otherwise, it may not be relevant for comparison.	3.99	4.45	5.62	7.44	

Example 3

In our third and final example, we will be focusing on selecting the top-performing fund within the small-cap category. As customary, we have identified 4 funds – ABC, DEF, GHI, and JKL – based on their respective 4 and 5-star ratings provided by Value Research and Morningstar. Now, our objective is to thoroughly compare these funds, considering various risk parameters and other pertinent factors. It's worth noting that an optimal AUM (Assets Under Management) size for a small-cap fund typically falls within the range of 1000 crore to 4000 crore.

Sl. No	Different parameters	Name of the funds				My preference
		ABC	DEF	GHI	JKL	
1.	AUM (in Cr.)	6,202	2,154	3,366	10,398	
2.	Alpha	5.80	5.77	10.28	2.46	
3.	Beta	0.87	0.94	0.78	0.96	
4.	Expense ratio	0.7	0.9	0.3	1.16	
5.	Sharpe ratio	0.13	0.12	0.34	0.11	GHI
6.	Standard Deviation	26.48	28.25	24.43	28.78	
7.	Sortino	1.09	1.05	1.11	1.01	
8.	R2 (should be more than 80)	95.84	96.60	89.63	98.15	
9.	Drawdown (maximum)	-33.04	-37.49	-30.20	-42.97	ABC
10.	Turnover ratio	22	29	13.08	32	
11.	Style box	Style-G/Cap-S	Style-G/Cap-M	Style-G/Cap-S	Style-G/Cap-M	
12.	No of Stocks in a portfolio	51	69	59	134	

Sl. No	Different parameters	Name of the funds				My preference
		ABC	DEF	GHI	JKL	
13.	Exit load	1% for redemption within 12 months	1% for redemption within 12 months	1% for redemption within 12 months	1% for redemption within 12 months	
14.	Fund management	No recent change in management.	No recent change in management.	No recent change in management.	No recent change in management.	**DEF**
15.	Fund's past 05 years trailing returns in comparison with its benchmark	Good	Above average	Very good	Average	
16.	Rolling returns	Good	Above average	Very good	Average	

Sl. No	Different parameters	Name of the funds				My preference
		ABC	DEF	GHI	JKL	
17.	Fund's P/E ratio (only if all the above mentioned funds follow same style of investing, whether it be growth or value. Otherwise, it may not be relevant for comparison.	32.99	35.52	29.06	36.11	JKL
18.	Fund's P/B ratio (only if all the above mentioned funds follow same style of investing, whether it be growth or value. Otherwise, it may not be relevant for comparison.	4.26	4.68	3.16	4.74	

Chapter

Understanding Mutual Fund NAV

NAV
NET ASSET VALUE

a) **The NAV isn't the price, so you shouldn't compare funds based on it.**

- The Net Asset Value (NAV) of a mutual fund represents the per-unit value of the fund's assets. However, it's important to understand that NAV isn't the same as the price you pay to buy or sell units of the fund. It's simply a calculation used to determine the value of each unit. Therefore, comparing mutual funds solely based on their NAV isn't a reliable way to assess their potential or performance.

b) **Getting more units with a lower NAV doesn't necessarily mean it's a better deal.**

- When a mutual fund has a lower NAV, you may receive more units for the same amount of money compared to a fund with a higher NAV. However, the number of units you own doesn't determine the quality of the investment. It's essential to consider other factors, such as the fund's investment objectives, past performance, expense ratio, and risk profile. Simply getting more units at a lower NAV doesn't guarantee better returns or benefits for the investor.

c) **A higher NAV doesn't guarantee better performance from the fund.**

- Some investors mistakenly believe that mutual funds with higher NAVs are superior investments. However, the NAV alone doesn't indicate how well a fund will perform in the future. Factors such as the fund's investment strategy, management team, market conditions, and underlying assets significantly influence its performance. Therefore, it's crucial not to assume that a fund with a high NAV will always outperform others. Investors should conduct thorough research and consider various factors before making investment decisions.

Chapter

Same-Day NAV for Mutual Fund Investments

It depends on the time we submit our application and transfer the money to the fund house. This is referred to as the cut-off time in a mutual fund, and it varies for different types of funds. Additionally, it depends on the chosen payment modes. The cut-off time for each third-party app differs. Therefore, it's essential to check their website before investing to ascertain their respective cut-off times.

Chapter

Dividends Received By a Mutual Fund

Subrata Das Gupta

DIVIDENDS

Equity mutual funds primarily invest in stocks of various companies, which mean they can receive dividends from these investments from time to time. While these dividends aren't directly transferred to investors' bank accounts, they still benefit investors indirectly.

When dividends are received, they are held as cash within the mutual fund. This cash influx temporarily increases the Assets under Management (AUM) and consequently impacts the Net Asset Value (NAV), causing it to rise.

However, this is a temporary parking of the dividends. Fund managers may strategically utilize this cash to seek out the best investment opportunities in the growth plan.

Chapter

Can Government Employee Invest in Share Market?

a) Can Government employees invest in the share market for the long term?

- Yes, if the total transaction in shares, mutual funds scheme, securities, debentures, etc., exceeds 6 months of basic pay of government servants during the calendar year, then intimation may be sent in the specific proforma to the concerned authority in respect of all government servants.

b) Can Government employees Trade in the share market?

- No.

c) Can someone else trade on behalf of a Government employee?

- No.

d) Can a Government employee trade on behalf of someone else?

- No.

e) Can a retired Government employee invest and trade in the share market?

- No.

Reference: As per the Central Civil Services (Conduct) Rules, 1964.

Chapter

24

Market Valuations, Investment Strategies and Portfolio Diversification

Valuation indicators				Market Valuations	What should an investor do	Number of funds in a portfolio	Proper fund Allocation between equity and debt based on the market valuations
Nifty 50 PE ratio	Nifty 50 PB ratio	Nifty Dividend yield ratio	Market cap to GDP ratio (Buffet indicator)				
< 18	<2.5	>1.8	50% -75%	Under valued	It's time to increase exposure to equity and decrease exposure to debt. Investors should consider investing more aggressively in fundamentally strong funds according to the prescribed ratio.	Total-06 (4-equity funds & 2- debt funds)	Allocate 70% of your investment to equities and 30% to debt instruments.
18-23	2.5-3.7	1.3-1.8	75%-90%	Fairly valued	It's time to maintain an equal exposure across both categories.	- DO -	Invest 50% in equities and 50% in debt.

>23	>4	<1.3	90%-120%	Over valued	Investors may consider booking partial profits and transitioning toward debt instruments. It's prudent to increase exposure to debt while reducing exposure to equity in accordance with the prescribed ratio. It's crucial to recognize that markets tend to correct after reaching extreme levels. However, exiting entire investments solely for profit booking might not be advisable, as determining the next opportune entry point can be challenging for many investors.	- DO -	Allocate 30% of your investment to equities and 70% to debt instruments.

Chapter

Knowing When to Exit from Mutual Funds

A) Achieving Financial Goals: If you reach your financial goals earlier than anticipated, it might be wise to exit from the Mutual Fund. Avoid being overly greedy. Alternatively, when you achieve 70-80 percent of your goal, consider transitioning the profit portion to less volatile asset classes such as short-term debt funds or fixed deposits to mitigate market volatility.

B) Inconsistent Fund Performance: If the fund consistently underperforms compared to its benchmark, it warrants attention. Allow sufficient time, at least one and a half years, for the fund to perform. If performance does not improve within this timeframe, consider switching to another fund.

C) Change in Fund Manager: The success of some Mutual Funds hinges significantly on their fund managers. It's crucial to assess the details of fund managers, including their past performance and previous experiences, as a change in fund manager can impact the fund's performance.

D) Due to a change in the fund's investment objective.

Chapter

Inflation and Investment Impact

- Inflation, simply put, means that over time, the prices of goods and services tend to increase. This means that the same amount of money will buy you fewer things in the future compared to what it could buy you in the past.

How does inflation affect our savings and investments?

- Every uptick in prices impacts our cost of living, eroding the value of our savings and investments. As inflation rises, the portion of our income saved or invested each month may not increase at the same rate. Consequently, the inflationary pressures exert additional strain on our savings and investments. Over time, due to the effects of inflation, the amount we've saved will purchase fewer goods.

How do we mitigate the impact of inflation?

- Various investment options can help counteract the effects of inflation. These include investing in stocks, mutual funds, bonds, real estate, gold, life insurance, tax-saving schemes, and more. These investments have the potential to not only grow your savings but also serve as a hedge against inflation.

Chapter

CAGR VS XIRR

XIRR VS CAGR

How to calculate CAGR using the RATE function in Excel

CAGR stands for Compound annual growth rate. It is the best tool to know your rate of return from a lumpsum investment over a period of time. The formula for calculating CAGR is:

$$= \textbf{RATE(nper,pmt,pv,-fv)}$$

- **Nper**: This represents the total number of periods.

- Pmt means if you have made some payments in between, which is in this case is zero. In case of CAGR calculation using rate function, pmt should always be zero (0).

- **Pv**: Pv denotes the present value of your investment.

- **Fv** signifies the future value, which must always be represented as a negative value for accurate calculation.

Let's run an equation using the sample table below where nper is 5. pv is 100, and fv is 500.

	A	B	C
1	**Total number of periods (nper)**	**Present Value (pv)**	**Future Value (fv)**
2	5	100	500
3			
4			
5			

a) Choose the cell in your spreadsheet where you wish to compute the Compound Annual Growth Rate (CAGR). For example, let's select cell B5.

b) Next, input the RATE formula into the chosen cell and specify the cell references containing your values. Remember to represent the future value as negative to prevent encountering an error message.

This is what my formula looks like.

	A	**B**	**C**
1	**Total number of periods (nper)**	**Present Value (pv)**	**Future Value (fv)**
2	5	100	500
3			
4			
5		**= RATE (A2, 0, B2, –C2)**	

c) Hit the enter button and run your equation. Using the sample data, my CAGR is 37.97%.

Limitation of CAGR: - It doesn't account for investment volatility.

How to calculate XIRR in Excel

Investing in mutual fund schemes via SIP or redeeming units through the Systematic Withdrawal Plan (SWP) is common practice. Given the multiple cash flows involved, using CAGR to determine returns from mutual funds isn't suitable. Instead, XIRR proves effective in calculating returns from mutual funds through SIP (incorporating multiple cash flows from SIP and top-ups) and SWP (encompassing various cash flows like dividends, partial redemptions, etc.).

The XIRR formula, a variation of IRR (Internal Rate of Return), accommodates irregular periods. To calculate SIP returns accurately, input SIP transactions and their corresponding dates from mutual fund statements into an Excel sheet. Then, apply the XIRR formula.

For instance, consider investing Rs 4,000 monthly in a mutual fund scheme through SIP. You can compute mutual fund returns via SIP using the XIRR Formula in Excel, as illustrated below.

	A	B	C	D	E	F
1	SIP Transaction Dates	Cash Flows				
2	20-07-2017	-4000				
3	20-08-2017	-4000				
4	20-09-2017	-4000				
5	20-10-2017	-4000				
6	20-11-2017	-4000				
7	20-12-2017	-4000				
8	20-01-2018	-4000				
9	20-02-2018	-4000				
10	20-03-2018	-4000				
11	20-04-2018	-4000				
12	20-05-2018	-4000				
13	20-06-2018	-4000				
14	20-07-2018	49000	**Redemption**			
15	**XIRR**	**=XIRR (B2: B14, A2: A14)**				

- All amounts you've invested, including SIP installments and additional repurchases, must be entered with a 'negative' sign.

- Redemption amounts must be entered with a 'positive' sign.

- In an Excel sheet, input SIP transaction dates in Column A.

- Subsequently, record the SIP installment as a negative figure in Column B.

- Against the redemption date, input the redemption amount in Column B.

Utilize the XIRR formula incorporating values, dates, and an optional guess value. For instance, input the formula =XIRR(B2:B14, A2:A14) and press enter. With the provided sample data, the XIRR is 3.88%.

Chapter

Retirement Corpus Management

1. **Collect Funds:** Collect all savings (like EPF, Gratuity, PPF, etc) that have been accumulated while on the job. Maintain a separate account for any remaining liabilities/ responsibilities, if you have any, such as expenses related to the child's marriage, the child's higher education, buying a home, etc. Do not merge this with your retirement fund. For instance, if you have a total savings of 60 lakh rupees after retirement and you need 20 lakh rupees for any of the aforementioned obligations, ensure that the 20 lakh rupees are kept in a separate account.

2. **Know your safe withdrawal rate:** In my opinion, despite estimating expenses after retirement, one has to focus on how much they should withdraw from their retirement corpus and then adjust the expenses accordingly. A US-based

financial adviser, William P. Bengen, first articulated the 4% withdrawal rate. According to him, the 4% is the percentage you could "safely" withdraw from a tax-advantaged portfolio in the first year of retirement, with the expectation you would live for 25 years in retirement & subsequently withdrawing based on inflation. If you withdraw too much too fast, you'll risk running out of money. Not withdrawing enough money can deny you the full benefit of your hard-earned savings.

3. **Building an Emergency Fund:** It's advisable to maintain an emergency fund equivalent to 6 months' worth of our expenses. This fund should be easily accessible and can be kept in a savings bank account or a liquid fund.

4. **Get Health Insurance:** A significant number of elderly individuals in India

depend on fixed monthly incomes like pensions, which might not cover unexpected medical expenses. Health insurance can provide essential financial support in such situations, easing the burden of medical costs.

Chapter

Investing Your Retirement Corpus

After retirement, it's wise to avoid taking risks or trying out new ways to invest your money. Most retired men in India only have a small amount of savings. Plus, they might not know much about different ways to invest or the risks involved. For these individuals, it's best to handle their retirement savings carefully.

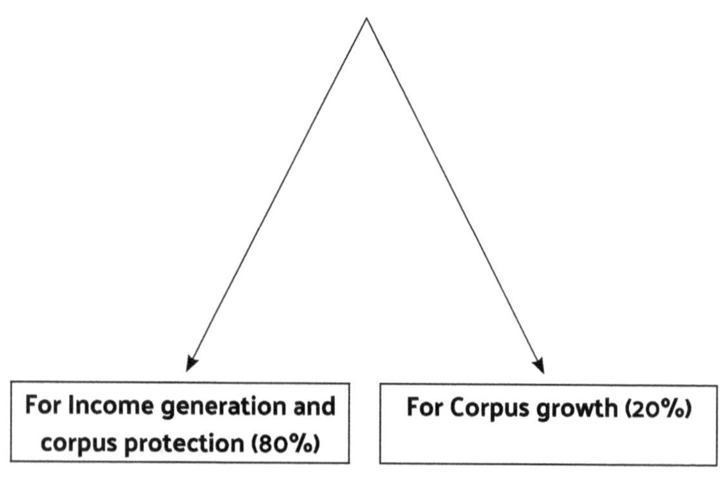

➢ SCSS (Senior Citizen Savings Scheme).	➢ Hybrid Scheme (Conservative hybrid fund & Balanced advantage fund)
➢ PO-MIS (Post Office – Monthly Income Scheme).	➢ Equity Oriented (Large cap fund
➢ Debt Mutual funds (Banking & PSU fund. ➢ Dynamic bond fund and Corporate bond fund) etc.	It's not recommended to invest your entire corpus in any equity fund in one go. Instead, spread the investment over 12 equal monthly installments through a Systematic Investment Plan (SIP) or a Systematic Transfer Plan (STP). This way, by investing gradually, you can average the purchase cost and lower the risk of investing when the market is at a high point. However, it's recommended to wait for at least two years before initiating an SWP in an equity scheme to benefit from capital appreciation and avoid Short-Term Capital Gains (STCG) tax, which is at a rate of 15%.

Chapter

Retirement Planning Calculator in Excel

Retirement Planning

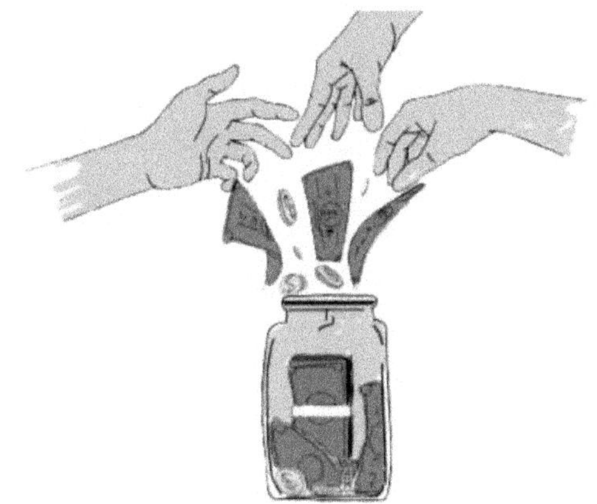

Retirement Planning calculator	
Current Age	Your age now
Current monthly expenses**(pv)**	The expenses that we incur every month.
Desired retirement age	The age at which we want to retire
No of years remaining for retirement **(npr)**	=Desired retirement age (-) Current age
Life expectancy	Age until which we expect to live
% expenses after retirement	80% (because usually when we stop earning, we cut down our expenses a bit).
Inflation rate (%)	we can consider an average of 5 to 6 percent inflation rate in India
Value of monthly expenses post retirement **(fv)**	=fv(rate,nper,0,-pv)* percentage expenses after retirement.
Life post-retirement	=Life expectancy (-) Desired retirement age
Post-retirement investment return	We should not expect more than 10% return here.
Amount required for retirement	=pv((expected return on investment (-) Expected inflation rate)/12,Life post retirement*12,-fv,0,1)

Note:

1) **Current monthly expenses:** - Exclude expenses such as home loan or rent payments, as they are unlikely to persist post-retirement. Include a component for medical expenses if not already accounted for.

2) **Inflation rate:** Refer to www.mospi.gov. in for All India inflation rates (%) based on CPI (General) and CFPI. Consider an average inflation rate of 5 to 6 percent in India.

3) **Post-retirement investment return:** - Keep in mind that our post-retirement portfolio will be dominated by debt-based fixed income investments and not equity.

4) **Life expectancy:** Determine the age until which we expect to live or until

which we anticipate our retirement corpus to last.

Chapter

Understanding SWP (Systematic Withdrawal Plan)

Systematic Withdrawal Plan
(SWP)
AMC
BANK

Systematic Withdrawal Plan (SWP) enables investors to withdraw fixed amounts at regular intervals, such as monthly, quarterly, half-yearly, or yearly, from their investments in any mutual fund scheme. This approach allows investors to generate both monthly income and accumulate a sum by the end of the maturity period. SWP proves particularly beneficial for retirees and senior citizens who rely on a steady monthly financial inflow. To grasp the concept better, one can utilize Groww's user-friendly SWP calculator, which is easily accessible online. The withdrawal amount can be tailored according to individual requirements. It's important to set up SWP carefully if one intends to preserve the capital. Withdrawals should ideally be less than the expected return to ensure capital preservation. Instead of investing the entire corpus in one go, it's advisable to spread the investment over 12 equal monthly installments through a Systematic Investment Plan (SIP) or a Systematic Transfer Plan (STP). This staggered approach helps average the purchase cost and mitigate the risk of investing at market highs. However, it's recommended to wait for at least 2 years before initiating a SWP in an equity scheme to benefit from capital appreciation and avoid the Short-Term Capital Gains (STCG) tax. While investors can deploy their entire corpus at once in a debt fund, the following mutual fund categories are well-suited for SWP:

a) Conservative Hybrid (Hybrid scheme)

b) Dynamic Asset Allocation/Balanced Advantage Fund (Hybrid scheme)

c) Large-Cap Fund (Equity oriented)

d) Banking and PSU Fund (Debt fund)

e) Corporate Bond Fund (Debt fund)

f) Dynamic Bond Fund (Debt fund)

Chapter

SWP Calculator with inflation in excel

Investment Insights

Initial investment amount (Rs.)	The lump-sum amount you want to invest in a mutual fund.	Input
Expected interest rate on corpus (%)	You should not expect more than a 10% return here, which is not difficult to generate by taking on only a slightly higher level of calculated risk. Bear in mind that our post-retirement portfolio will be dominated by debt-based fixed income investments, with very little equity, as SWP is mostly beneficial for retirees and senior citizens.	Input
Expected Average Inflation rate (%)	You can consider an average inflation rate of 6 percent in India. However, if you opt for a high inflation rate, the expected interest rate on your corpus must also be high, which is not favorable for retirees and senior citizens. Conversely, considering a low inflation rate of less than 4 percent can impact your purchasing power after retirement.	Input
SWP Duration	How long you want to continue the SWP?	Input
First year withdrawal rate (%)	Should not be more than 4%	Input
Year wise monthly withdrawal (Rs.)	=VLOOKUP(lookup_value,table_array,col_index_num,0)	Output
Inflation adjusted total yearly withdrawal (Rs)	=VLOOKUP(lookup_value,table_array,col_index_num,0)	Output
Final Value	=VLOOKUP(lookup_value,table_array,col_index_num,0)	Output

Note:

a) **Expected Interest Rate on Corpus:** You should not expect more than a 10% return here, which is not difficult to generate by taking on only a slightly higher level of calculated risk. Bear in mind that our post-retirement portfolio will be dominated by debt-based fixed income investments with very little equity, as SWP is mostly beneficial for retirees and senior citizens.

b) **Expected Average Inflation Rate:** You need to visit www.mospi.gov.in to learn about all India inflation rates (%) based on CPI (General) and CFPI. You can consider an average inflation rate of 6 percent in India. However, if you opt for a high inflation rate, the expected interest rate on your corpus must also be high, which is not favorable for retirees and senior citizens. Conversely, considering a low inflation rate of less than 4 percent can impact your purchasing power after retirement.

c) **First Year Withdrawal Rate:** A US-based financial adviser, William P. Bengen, first articulated the 4% withdrawal rate. According to him, the 4% is the percentage you could "safely" withdraw from a tax-advantaged portfolio in the first year of retirement, with the expectation you would live for 25 years in retirement & subsequently withdrawing based on inflation. If you withdraw too much too fast, you'll risk running out of money. Not withdrawing enough money can deny you the full benefit of your hard-earned savings.

d) **Final Value:** In order to get the year wise monthly withdrawal, Inflation adjusted total yearly withdrawal and final value of your investment based on SWP duration; you can use 'VLOOKUP' formula here with the help of SWP calculation sheet.

SWP Calculation sheet

Year	Op. Balance	Yearly Initial SWP	Inflation adjusted total yearly withdrawal	Year wise monthly withdrawal	Earnings	Cl. Balance
1.	= Initial investment amount	= Op. Balance * First year withdrawal rate /100	= Yearly Initial SWP	= Inflation adjusted total yearly withdrawal/ 12	= Op. Balance * Expected interest rate on corpus/100	= Op. Balance (+) Earnings (-) Inflation adjusted total yearly withdrawal
2.	= Previous year Cl. Balance	Here amount will be same in each row	= Previous year Inflation adjusted total yearly withdrawal * (Expected Average Inflation rate/100) + Previous year Inflation adjusted total yearly withdrawal	Drag the above formula	Drag the above formula	Drag the above formula
3.	Drag the above formula	-do-	Drag the above formula	-do-	-do-	-do-

4.	-do-	-do-	-do-	-do-	-do-	-do-
5.	-do-	-do-	-do-	-do-	-do-	-do-
6.	-do-	-do-	-do-	-do-	-do-	-do-
7.	-do-	-do-	-do-	-do-	-do-	-do-
8.	-do-	-do-	-do-	-do-	-do-	-do-
9.	-do-	-do-	-do-	-do-	-do-	-do-
10.	-do-	-do-	-do-	-do-	-do-	-do-
11.	-do-	-do-	-do-	-do-	-do-	-do-
12.	-do-	-do-	-do-	-do-	-do-	-do-
13.	-do-	-do-	-do-	-do-	-do-	-do-
14.	-do-	-do-	-do-	-do-	-do-	-do-
15.	-do-	-do-	-do-	-do-	-do-	-do-
16.	-do-	-do-	-do-	-do-	-do-	-do-
17.	-do-	-do-	-do-	-do-	-do-	-do-
18.	-do-	-do-	-do-	-do-	-do-	-do-
19.	-do-	-do-	-do-	-do-	-do-	-do-
20.	-do-	-do-	-do-	-do-	-do-	-do-

Chapter

Understanding Front Running and its Punishment

FRONT RUNNING

- Frontrunning is an illegal practice in which an individual or broker gains advanced knowledge of a significant transaction set to occur in a specific stock. Prior to executing the trade, the broker invests in the stock through a personal account, anticipating a favorable price movement. For instance, imagine a scenario where a broker receives a substantial order to buy 6,000,000 shares of a company trading at 200 rupees per share. Before executing the order, the broker purchases 30,000 shares of the same company in their personal capacity. Subsequently, when the broker executes the large trade, the share price increases to 203 rupees, enabling the broker to sell their shares at a profit.

Punishment: Any individual who indulges in fraudulent and unfair trade practices shall be liable with a penalty which may extend to 25 crore rupees or 3 times the profit made out of such practices, whichever is higher.

Chapter

Abbreviations in Mutual Funds

AUM- Asset under Management

AMC- Asset Management Company

EPS- Earnings per Share

FI- Financial Institutions

FII- Foreign Institutional Investor

NAV- Net Asset Value

MF- Mutual Funds

MF- Money Market Mutual Funds

FOF- Funds of Funds

NBFC- Non-Banking Finance Company

NPA- Non-Performing Asset

NFO- New Fund offer

P/E, PER- Price/ Earnings Ratio.

ROC- Registrar of Companies

SEBI- Securities and Exchange Board of India

YTM- Yield to Maturity

SIP- Systematic Investment Plan

SWP- Systematic Withdrawal Plan

STP- Systematic Transfer Plan

ARN- AMFI Registration Number

CP- Commercial Paper

FRB- Floating Rate Bond

T- Bills- Treasury Bills

PSUB- Public Sector Undertaking Bonds

TM- Term to Maturity

ICRA- Information and Credit Rating Agency

CRISIL- Credit Ratings and Information Services (India) Ltd.

CQR- Credit Quality Rating.

RAR- Risk-Adjusted Return

STCG- Short-Term Capital Gain

LTCG- Long-Term Capital Gain

ELSS- Equity Linked Saving Schemes

CAP- Capitalization

SEC- Securities Exchange Commission

AMFI- Association of Mutual Funds in India

Chapter

Q&A Session

1. What is the recommended frequency for portfolio rebalancing?

   - Once annually, typically on a calendar year basis.

2. Is it possible to accurately predict the stock market's movements?

   - Timing the stock market reliably is considered unfeasible.

3. How many mutual funds are typically recommended for achieving diversification in a portfolio?

   - A diversified portfolio may consist of around 6 funds, including 4 equity funds and 2 debt funds.

4. Which platform can be used to access rolling returns data for mutual funds?

- Advisorkhoj.com offers rolling returns data for mutual funds.

5. Where can investors find information on the overlap of mutual fund portfolios?

- Thefundoo.com provides insights into mutual fund portfolio overlap.

6. What level of portfolio overlap is generally considered acceptable?

- A maximum overlap of 30% between schemes is typically considered acceptable.

7. What is a realistic expectation for the average annual return from equity mutual fund investments with a horizon exceeding 6 years?

- Investors can expect a maximum average annual return of 15%.

8. How can investors access the current PE, PB, and Dividend yield ratios of the Nifty 50?

- Information on the current PE, PB, and Dividend yield ratios of the Nifty 50 can be found on www.niftyindices.com